Why Are People Terrorists?

Alex Woolf

Raintree
Chicago, Illinois

© 2005 Raintree
Published by Raintree
a division of Reed Elsevier, Inc.
Chicago, Ilinois
Customer Service 888-363-4266
Visit our website at www.raintreelibrary.com

Library of Congress Cataloging-in-Publication Data
Woolf, Alex.
  Why are people terrorists? / Alex Woolf.
    p. cm. -- (Exploring tough issues)
Summary: Explores issues related to terrorism, such as who becomes a
terrorist and why, and options such as the "War Against Terrorism" for
fighting against these acts of violence agains innocent people.
Includes bibliographical references and index.
  ISBN 0-7398-6686-9 (lib. bdg. : alk. paper)
  1. Terrorism--Juvenile literature. [1. Terrorism.] I. Title. II.
Series.
  HV6431.W626 2005
  303.6'25--dc22

2003011571

08 07 06 05 04
10 9 8 7 6 5 4 3 2 1
Printed by C&C Offset, China.

Picture acknowledgments
The publisher would like to thank the following for permission to reproduce photographs: pp. 4, 9 Popperfoto (AFP, André Durand); pp. 5, 13, 14, 15, 16, 29, 21, 23, 24, 25, 33, 34, 36, 38, 39, 40, 42 Popperfoto/Reuters: 5 (Antony Njuguna), 13 (Jamal Saidi), 14 (Dylan Martinez), 15 (Reinhard Krause), 16 (Win McNamee), 20 (Dan Chung), 21 (Yannis Behrakis), 23 (Lee Jae-won), 24 (Jose Miguel Gomez), 25, 33 (Sharif Karim), 34 (U.S. DoD), 36 (British MoD), 38 (Sean Adair), 39 (Shannon Stapleton), 40 (Vasily Fedosenko), 42 (Portland Police Dept.); p. 6 Hodder Wayland Picture Library; pp. 7,8, 26, 27, 28, 35, 37, 44 Corbis; pp. 10, 12, 29, 31, 45 Rex Features: 10, 12 (Reardon), 29 (Sipa Press, Jon Mitchell), 31 (Sipa Press), 45; p. 11 Impact (Philippe Achache); pp. 17, 30 Topham/AP; p.18 Camera Press; p. 19 Topham Picture Point; p. 22 Topham/ImageWorks; p. 32 Topham/Press Association; pp. 41, 43 Getty Images: 41 (Joe Raedle), 43 (Eric Miller).

Cover picture: Corbis
September 11, 2001. The World Trade Center in New York is hit by al-Qaeda terrorists.

Contents

1. What Is Terrorism?

What does terrorism mean?

Terrorism is the deliberate use of violence against innocent people to inspire fear for political purposes. It is often the work of small groups who want power. They might want to change the way their country is governed, or to change the world in a political or religious way. Terrorism can also be used by governments against people and groups that they view as dangerous.

Most groups who use political violence do not call themselves terrorists. They prefer to describe themselves in different ways—for example, as revolutionaries fighting against a brutal government. The government may call them terrorists, but the group might claim that they are the real victims of terrorist acts committed by the people in power.

"I consider those actions as a means of spreading our cause. A small group is eliminated, but a great humanity will be created in its place."
Abdullah Ocalan, leader of the terrorist group PKK (Kurdish Workers' Party), replying to the accusation that his actions have resulted in the deaths of women and children.

◀ *In October 2002 Russian special forces stormed a theater in Moscow to free hostages held by Chechen rebel fighters who had threatened to kill the hostages if the rebels' political demands were not met. The Chechens and more than a hundred hostages died in the rescue.*

People have many different opinions about the actions of terrorists, and even what terrorism is. Many people in the world believe that all acts of political violence, whatever the cause, are unacceptable, and should be called terrorism. However, there are also a large number of people who support the aims of the people who commit these violent acts. They believe violent methods are an acceptable way of changing the way a country is ruled. They would not call themselves, or those carrying out the acts, terrorists.

▲ *In November 2002 three suspected Al Qaeda terrorists crashed a car containing explosives into a hotel near Mombasa, Kenya, where Israeli tourists were on vacation. Three Israeli tourists and ten Kenyans were killed.*

The history of terrorism

The government itself could practice terrorism during the French Revolution, because it had the backing of thousands of Parisians. Here an angry mob hangs a hated politician of the former government from a lamppost in a Paris square in July 1789.

The word "terrorism" was first used in English in 1795 to describe the actions of the French government during the Reign of Terror (1793–1794). This was a very violent stage of the French Revolution, when hundreds of people suspected of being against the revolution were beheaded by guillotine. Terrorism had been used before this time, by governments and small groups, but this was the first time that it was recognized as a political strategy.

During the later 19th and early 20th centuries, terrorism became a favorite weapon of some anarchists—those who believed in overthrowing all governments by force. These groups killed or threatened officials and politicians across Europe and the United States.

FACT:
Between 1894 and 1914, anarchists in Western Europe and the United States caused the deaths of six heads of state including U.S. President William McKinley, who was shot by Leon Czolgosz in September 1901.

During the late 1940s, terrorist groups sprang up in many countries controlled by foreign powers, such as French Algeria and Indochina. These groups used violence against the troops and officials of the foreign power and tried to force them out. These terrorists were called nationalist terrorists because they wanted their homeland or "nation" back under their control.

Terrorism became more widespread in the late 1960s. Many people had lost faith in their governments and felt that society was basically unfair. Political extremists formed terrorist groups in countries across Europe, the Americas, and Asia hoping to overthrow their governments by bomb attacks, shootings, and hijackings. Since the 1980s the nationalists and political extremists have been joined by religious extremists, particularly certain Muslim groups. They are now the major force behind terrorism in the world.

▼ A department store in Lebanon is wrecked by a bomb explosion during a 1958 rebellion by left-wing Muslim, Marxist terrorists against the pro-Western, Christian government.

Sometimes governments have used terror to control their people. State terrorism was practiced from the 1920s to the 1940s by the Bolsheviks in the Soviet Union and by the fascist governments of Germany and Italy. These regimes formed secret police forces, and imprisoned and tortured those suspected of antigovernment activities. Modern governments that have used state terrorism include the former government of Saddam Hussein in Iraq, and the military regime that controls Myanmar (Burma).

The aim of terrorism

There are three basic aims behind nearly all terrorist attacks. The first is to advertise the terrorist group and its cause. When there is a bomb attack in a public place, or a well-known politician is assassinated, people want to know who has done it, and why. These acts can give a small group major publicity in the newspapers and on television all around the world, even if only for a short time.

The second aim of terrorist activity is to destroy the peace of a country, and to make its government feel insecure and worried. Terrorists choose their targets carefully to cause the maximum disruption and disorder. They may, for example, choose to put a bomb in a shopping mall, a railroad station, or a government building. In addition to the political damage this can cause, terrorists also hope to cause economic damage. For example, they may scare away tourists or businesses thinking of investing money in a country.

▶ *An Algerian soldier in the French army guards a group of captured FLN (National Liberation Front) terrorists. During the 1950s the FLN fighters struggled to liberate Algeria from French rule.*

▲ One of the main aims of terrorist attacks is to cause fear. Here people stand around in shock at the site of a car-bomb explosion in a Jerusalem market in 1998.

The third aim of terrorism is to provoke a government into behaving harshly. Faced with terrorist attacks, a government might strengthen the powers of its police force to arrest and question suspects. It may limit freedom of speech and movement to stop terrorists from recruiting more supporters. By imposing strict controls on the entire country, the government will often make itself unpopular, and the terrorists may get sympathy or support as a result.

> "People refuse to collaborate [deal] with the authorities, and the general sentiment is that the government is unjust, incapable of solving problems, and resorts purely and simply to the physical liquidation [destruction] of its opponents."
>
> *Brazilian terrorist Carlos Marighella describing what can happen when a government overreacts to terrorism*

Terrorism and the media

Terrorists take advantage of the media. Terrorist actions reported on television and radio and in the newspapers can give terrorist groups wide exposure and the power to put pressure on governments. So why does the press go on reporting terrorist attacks?

First, journalists are always on the lookout for a dramatic news story, and few events are more dramatic or newsworthy than a terrorist hijacking or bombing. Second, most people working in the media believe that people have a right to know what is going on in the world. Third, there is a danger that a government might try to stop the media from reporting "terrorist" acts as a way of silencing its opponents. As we have seen, terrorism can mean different things to different people, and it is a useful label to apply to one's enemies. Journalists naturally object to the idea that they should not report any antigovernment attack or protest.

▶ *The terrorists involved in the attacks on September 11, 2001, certainly got publicity. The event made headlines around the world for several days.*

◀ *The media is naturally drawn to dramatic stories. For six days in 1980, the siege of London's Iranian embassy by an Iranian terrorist group was played out in the full glare of publicity. A TV audience of millions watched as British troops stormed the embassy and rescued the hostages.*

Terrorists try to exploit the free publicity available from the world's media. However, they have no control over how their actions are presented. News stories usually concentrate more on their violence than the cause they are trying to publicize. So terrorists use other ways to advertise themselves. Leaflets and newspapers are often printed to explain their aims and ideals. Now the Internet provides terrorists with an easy way of reaching a worldwide audience directly. Some terrorist groups, such as the Lebanese Hezbollah, even run their own radio and TV stations, letting them communicate directly with their intended audiences.

“Whichever way one looks at it, the situation in our country is deeply worrying. The two States [France and Spain] have always used all their instruments—military, political, economic, and cultural—to destroy this nation's resources to be free in the future.... They consider us their enemies instead of neighbors and prefer to oppress this nation rather than to respect the voice of Basque people in a peaceful way.”

Excerpt from a 1998 press release from ETA, a terrorist group fighting in Spain for an independent Basque state

2. Why do People Become Terrorists?

The power of nationalism

One reason terrorism might occur is if a group of people within a country hold very different beliefs from those in power. They are often unhappy with the way they are governed and have stong feelings about their national identity. This group may be unable to further its cause through democratic means, such as by voting for a change of government. Often there are a few people in these groups who are willing to take violent action.

Nationalist terrorism can arise in a group of people with a common ethnic or cultural identity who wish to form their own nation. In the same way, people who were once free, but whose land is occupied by a conquering power, may be inspired to fight for their independence.

Examples of this include the Liberation Tigers of Tamil Eelam (LTTE). The Tamil are a people without their own country who live in southern India and northern Sri Lanka. Since the early 1970s, the LTTE have carried out bombings and assassinations as part of a campaign to win the Tamil an independent state within Sri Lanka.

▼ *Terrorist groups often find willing recruits among young men and even boys. A young member of the Tamil Tigers is shown here armed with an assault rifle.*

The Kurds are another people without their own country. They live mostly in Turkey and Iraq. Iraqi Kurds in particular have suffered because they do not have an independent homeland. They were attacked with biological and chemical weapons by the Iraqi army of Saddam Hussein. The aim of the Kurdish Workers' Party (PKK) is to establish an independent Kurdistan. They have carried out many assassinations and bomb attacks in Turkey.

case study·case study·case study·case study·case study

Ahmad is a 27-year-old Palestinian living with his mother and eight brothers and sisters in Gaza, an area under Israeli control. Ahmad has been raised to believe that his mother's family was unjustly forced out of Jaffa in 1948 when Israel was established and he believes he is treated as a "second-class citizen" in what he sees as his own country. Because he has never been given any reason to hope for change, he has joined the al-Aqsa Martyrs Brigades, a group fighting for a Palestinian state. The Brigade was responsible for several murderous suicide attacks against innocent civilians in 2002. Ahmad says he prefers to die in a suicide attack than continue to live as a second-class citizen.

Political beliefs

Many terrorists decide to take action because they disagree with the values or policies of those in power, both in their own country and around the world. A simplified approach to discussing political terrorists is to divide them into two major groups: left-wing and right-wing.

Left-wing terrorist groups generally believe that the free enterprise economic system, in which industry is controlled by private owners for profit, is the main cause of world poverty. Many left-wing terrorists favor another system, known as communism, in which all wealth and property is

▲ Some people think that globalization and the increasing power of international business are the main causes of world poverty. A demonstrator is seen here throwing a gas bomb at a rally protesting globalization in 2001.

case study•case study•case study•case study•case study

Ulrike Meinhof was born in 1934 in Oldenburg, Germany. As a university student she became involved in the antinuclear movement, and went on to become a respected left-wing journalist. Her political views grew more extreme after she interviewed the communist Andreas Baader while he was in prison for arson. She grew to believe that violence was the only way to change society. In May 1970 she helped to free Baader from prison, and together with Baader's girlfriend they formed a terrorist group called the Red Army Faction, also known as the Baader-Meinhof Gang. For the next two years they carried out a wave of brutal terrorist acts across West Germany, including the bombings of office buildings, police stations, and U.S. Army bases. Meinhof was arrested in 1972 and sentenced to eight years of prison. She committed suicide in 1976 while still in prison.

controlled by the state. There were many left-wing terrorist groups born in the late 1960s in capitalist Europe and North America. They included the Red Brigades in Italy, Baader-Meinhof in West Germany, Direct Action in France, and the Weathermen in the United States.

Right-wing terrorists want to keep traditional ways of life, which they think are threatened by social changes. They often blame social change on immigrants from other ethnic groups. They are usually fiercely patriotic and often racist. Examples include the Ku Klux Klan in the United States, the National Democratic Party in Germany, and other supremacist groups who believe in the superiority of their own group and preach hatred of others. As economic conditions began to worsen in the late 1990s, these groups began to gain political power, particularly in France and Germany.

▼ *Extreme right-wing groups, such as the National Democratic Party (NPD) of Germany, are a continuing—if small-scale— political force in many European countries. These NPD supporters are taking part in a demonstration in Leipzig, Germany, in 1998.*

Religious reasons

Religious fundamentalists do not believe that religion should be a matter of personal choice. They feel the laws and government of their country should be based on their interpretations of the holy book of their religion, for example, the Christian Bible or the Muslim Koran.

In the United States, most religious fundamentalists are Christian. Some have turned to terrorism on a small scale, including the bombing of abortion clinics. In Japan a religious sect called Aum Shinrikyo has emerged as a reaction against the decline of traditional Japanese culture. Attacks on Israel have led to the rise of Jewish fundamentalist terrorist groups such as Kach and Kahane Chai, who carry out attacks on the Israeli government and on Palestinians in the occupied territories.

One of the most serious terrorist threats facing the world today is Islamic terrorism. This threat first

◀ *Religious extremists like to stress their purity. They urge others to find salvation by repenting their sins and praying. This demonstrator at a religious rally in Washington, D.C., claims he is wearing "the spiritual armor of God."*

▲ An anti-American demonstration in Iran in 1979. The placard on the left shows the Islamic fundamentalist Ayatollah Khomeini, who took power in Iran during that year.

emerged in 1979 when an Islamic fundamentalist regime came to power in Iran. Muslim fundamentalists are also known as Islamists. The Islamist victory in Iran inspired others in the Muslim world. Islamists encouraged other Muslims to try to change their own countries by attacking their "antireligious" governments.

The policy of Israel toward the Palestinians is also used by some Muslims as a justification for terrorism. Islamic terrorists also launch attacks on the non-Muslim West, especially the United States, for its support of Israel. They view the West as the source of the evil that has ruined their own countries.

> "The ruling to kill the Americans and their allies—civilians and military—is an individual duty for every Muslim who can do it in any country in which it is possible to do it ... in order for their armies to move out of all the lands of Islam, defeated and unable to threaten any Muslim...."
>
> *A fatwah [religious ruling] delivered by Islamic terrorist Osama bin Laden in 1998*

3. What Methods do Terrorists Use?

Hostage taking

Terrorists usually have few resources compared to the governments they fight against. They must choose their methods carefully to apply maximum pressure on their enemies. One very powerful way of doing this is to take hostages.

Hostage taking is often used by terrorists to make a statement about their cause to the world. It is also a means for the terrorists to raise money or supplies through ransom demands. Hostage dramas can drag on for weeks. This extends the time during which the terrorists are in the spotlight. When terrorists demand money or the release of prisoners, threatening human lives can also be a highly effective way of getting what they want.

◀ Brian Keenan (center) was held hostage in Lebanon for over four years, between 1986 and 1990, by the terrorist group Hezbollah. He is shown at a rally calling for the release of a fellow hostage, John McCarthy.

case study·case study·case study·case study·case study

On March 16, 1978 Aldo Moro, president of the conservative Christian Democrat Party of Italy, was kidnapped by the left-wing terrorist group, the Red Brigades, and was held hostage for 55 days. The terrorists demanded that their organization be recognized as a political party. They also demanded the release of 13 members of the Red Brigades, then on trial in Turin. The two ruling parties of Italy, the Christian Democrats and the Communists, refused to negotiate. After repeated threats by the Red Brigades, Aldo Moro was murdered on May 9, 1978.

In hostage situations terrorists often aim to increase the terror and panic of hostages to make them more submissive. One way of doing this is for one terrorist to appear violent and out of control, hitting hostages and shouting at them, while another is calm, soft-spoken, and reassuring. This technique was used by anti-Israel terrorists who hijacked an Air France flight in 1976. It was also used by supporters of an independent Croatia, who hijacked a TWA flight a few months later.

In order to increase the pressure on a government, hijackers will sometimes kill a hostage. In a hijacking by Islamic terrorists in June 1985, an American passenger was killed. Passengers with Israeli passports were herded into a separate area from the others and threatened with the same fate. The effect of these actions persuaded the American and Israeli governments to give in to the terrorists' demands.

▲ The politician Aldo Moro, who was imprisoned and later killed by the Red Brigades in Italy. This photograph was taken while he was being held hostage in 1978.

Murder and destruction

Terrorists sometimes try to shock governments into action by killing people or destroying property. One favored method is assassination—the killing of a single, well-known figure, often from the government or armed forces. The aim of assassination is to shock and undermine a government. It also shows that terrorists can strike anywhere, even at the heart of a government.

By choosing assassination terrorists are showing that they are not blind killers, but can select a target carefully. Rehavam Zeevi, a right-wing Israeli government minister, was assassinated by the Popular Front for the Liberation of Palestine in October 2001, specifically because of his extreme views.

Large bombs, usually planted in vehicles and powerful enough to destroy a building or devastate a street, are another method terrorists use to cause chaos, panic, and fear. Before a bomb attack some terrorist groups, such as the IRA and ETA, give a telephone warning. They do this to show that their aim is not to kill people but to destroy property and get attention.

▼ *The aftermath of the bomb blast at Omagh in Northern Ireland in which 28 people were killed.*

case study·case study·case study·case study·case study

On Saturday August 15, 1998, fourteen-year-old schoolgirl Una McGurk went with a friend for lunch into Omagh town center in Northern Ireland. There had been a bomb threat, and Una's friend left to telephone her parents to tell them she was safe. When the bomb, planted by the Real IRA, went off at 3:10 P.M., Una was just a few yards away from it. She heard the explosion, and then everything went black. She was knocked over, but got up again and began walking down the street. She saw dead bodies everywhere. She was drenched in blood yet didn't feel any pain. Una eventually collapsed and was rushed to a hospital where she remained for eight weeks, recovering from wounds to her feet, arms, legs, and torso. The scarring on her face was so bad that two years later she was still wearing a special plastic mask to help the tissue heal. For two years she suffered from depression, and still has recurring nightmares about that day.

Suicide bombers first appeared in the early 1980s. They are one of the most feared terrorist weapons because they are willing to give up their own lives and are hard to stop. Individuals wired with explosives hidden on their bodies are very difficult to detect. By positioning themselves in crowded places, like buses or restaurants, they can cause many deaths. They are most often used by Islamic terrorist groups, like Hamas and Hezbollah, against Israeli civilian targets.

▼ *A tag identifying a victim of a suicide bombing in Jerusalem in June 2002. Seventeen people were killed in the attack.*

Weapons of mass destruction

One alarming threat involves the use of weapons of mass destruction. These are chemical, biological, and nuclear weapons that can kill thousands of people. Chemical weapons release poisonous substances into the atmosphere that can injure or kill people. Biological weapons release bacteria or viruses that spread diseases among human, animal, and plant life. Nuclear weapons are very powerful bombs that kill people and destroy property for miles around the center of the blast. They also pollute the site with radioactivity that can sicken or kill people long after the bomb has first exploded.

FACT:
The first recorded use of a weapon of mass destruction by terrorists was the release of sarin, a highly poisonous nerve gas, in the Tokyo underground on March 20, 1995. The attack, which killed eleven and injured more than 5,000, was launched by the Japanese religious sect Aum Shinrikyo. They placed containers of the gas on a train during rush hour, and punctured them with umbrellas before leaving the train.

▶ *The scene following the sarin gas attack on the Tokyo subway in 1995. In 1999 a senior member of the cult responsible for the attack was sentenced to death.*

Chemical weapons are at their most deadly when used in a small area, such as a subway system. Both biological and chemical weapons could also be used to contaminate food or a city's water supply. Biological weapons have even been delivered by mail. In October 2001, letters containing spores of a deadly disease called anthrax were sent to several U.S. senators and to people in the media. Five people died as a result.

Nuclear weapons are complicated to make and use certain rare types of material. However, it is possible that after the collapse of the Soviet Union in 1991, some of that country's nuclear material and weapon-making ability was purchased or otherwise obtained by terrorists.

▲ *A South Korean family carries out a monthly civil defense drill. They are rehearsing the evacuation of a building in the event of a chemical attack.*

However, many believe that more danger comes not from a nuclear bomb, but from the use of nuclear material. A radioactive dispersal device (RDD), or "dirty bomb," is a conventional bomb surrounded by nuclear material. When it explodes, a dirty bomb spreads radioactive material in all directions. But it is difficult to obtain enough radioactive material to cause widespread damage. These bombs are not necessarily more dangerous than conventional terrorist bombs.

4. The Supporters of Terrorism

Where do terrorists get their money?

Terrorists raise money in many different ways. These include the proceeds of crime, such as bank robberies, kidnap ransoms, and drug dealing. They also use legal forms of fundraising, such as charity drives, business donations, and taxes on their supporters. Terrorists are also sometimes given money and other kinds of support by the governments of certain countries.

Islamic terrorist groups benefit from the Muslim custom of making regular charitable gifts, known as *zekath*, at mosques. Many of those who give money do not know that it may end up in the hands of terrorists. The Hamas group raises tens of millions of dollars a year through a network of charity associations operating in the Israeli-occupied territories, Europe, and the United States.

▶ *These are two members of the rebel National Liberation Army (ELN) of Colombia. The ELN now obtains most of its funds by helping producers of illegal drugs.*

ETA supporters in Spain hold a flag over the coffin of one of their former leaders. She was killed during a police raid in 1998. The group raises money through robbery, extortion (blackmailing), and drug smuggling.

Charitable gifts are the most important source of finance for al-Qaeda, another Islamic terrorist organization. Some of the charities through which it receives money are just front organizations that hide the real purpose of their fundraising. Others are genuine, but they have been infiltrated by al-Qaeda members. Al-Qaeda also makes money through legal businesses, such as Osama bin Laden's construction company in Sudan.

Nationalist terrorist groups such as ETA (Basque), PKK (Kurds), FARC (Colombia), and LTTE (Tamil) make most of their money through drug smuggling and donations from supporters. PKK makes about $86 million a year this way.

FACT:
The *hawala* underground banking system is a popular way for Islamic terrorists to transfer money to and from bank accounts in secrecy. There are no contracts or printed records that would give evidence of a money transfer, yet hundreds of thousands of dollars can move around the world in a matter of hours. Each person involved in the transfer receives a small commission for playing his or her part. As long as the different links in the chain trust one another, the money will move from one bank to another as desired.

States that support terrorism

Sometimes governments believe that it is in their interest to support terrorist groups, particularly when they have a common enemy. A country may not wish to go to war openly with another country, but terrorist organizations can provide a way for that goverment to attack an enemy indirectly. This is called state-supported terrorism.

This happened during the period of rivalry between the United States and the Soviet Union known as the Cold War (1945–1990). Many left-wing groups in Europe, Asia, and South America were given money and arms by the Soviet Union and its allies. In a similar way, the United States provided support and training for right-wing groups fighting left-wing governments in countries like Cuba, Nicaragua, and Chile.

◀ *These Contra rebels patrol the northern mountains of Nicaragua. The guerrilla forces battled the left-wing Sandinista government during the 1980s with support from the United States.*

> " Although it sponsors terrorism, Syria is always careful to seem to be against it. In this broadcast it identifies the Palestinians as freedom-fighters while accusing the Israeli forces sent against them of being the real terrorists: "Syria condemns terror and will continue to condemn it at every opportunity, but what Israel defines as terror is national struggle against occupation.... The Israeli occupation of the territories and collective punishment that Israel imposes on the citizenry is terror."
>
> *Broadcast by Damascus Radio, 1996*

State-supported terrorism has declined since the end of the Cold War. The U.S. State Department lists several countries that currently sponsor terror. Most of these are Islamic nations. Iran, for example, gives about $3 million a year to the terrorist group Hamas and, it is believed, 10 times that amount to Hezbollah. Syria supports the Islamic groups the Abu Nidal Organization and the PFLP, and also provides help for the Kurdish nationalists, the PKK.

▲ *A member of Hamas protests the killing of one of his fellow members. Hamas is supported by a network of charity associations in Saudi Arabia and the Gulf States, as well as by Iran.*

Communist North Korea, also on the State Department list, has for many years carried out terrorist operations in foreign countries. In 1983, for example, North Korean agents blew up members of the Burmese government, and in 1988 they destroyed a South Korean airliner.

Terrorism and organized crime

Many terrorist organizations have turned to crime, and especially drug smuggling, to raise money. The drug trade is now the main method by which terrorists around the world get their money. This has led to a growing link between terrorist groups and international crime rings.

There are obvious differences between terrorist and traditional criminal groups. Terrorists are usually driven by political or religious goals. Criminals usually act out of greed. However, they have found ways of working together to benefit each other. For example, the left-wing Revolutionary Armed Forces of Colombia (FARC) and the National Liberation Army (ELN) of Colombia are paid large sums for providing armed security for powerful Colombian drug producers.

▼ *Peruvian army troops search a village in Ayacucho for "Shining Path" terrorists. Seven provinces in this area were placed under military control in 1982 in an effort to destroy this rebel force.*

Colombian antidrug police in the poppy fields of the Huila region carry out a raid on opium producers. Opium poppies are used to make drugs such as heroin.

This sort of work is far more profitable than other forms of fundraising, such as kidnapping and bank robberies—and far less risky. Terrorist groups can also make use of drug smuggling routes to move people and arms secretly into Western cities.

There are other advantages for both sides. Organized crime gangs are often able to bribe corrupt political leaders. Terrorist groups who wish to influence or threaten a government can make use of these people. Similarly, powerful terrorist groups can cause political unrest in countries and so weaken these governments, as they have done in places like Colombia and Afghanistan. This makes it easier for organized crime groups to operate without police or government interference.

> "The West is exporting to us its corrosive [destructive] culture. We are exporting something back that corrodes their society."
> *Islamic terrorist Osama bin Laden explaining al-Qaeda's involvement in the taxing, protection, and encouragement of the opium industry in Afghanistan*

5. What Can be Done About Terrorism?

Taking action against terrorism

Countries faced with terrorist attacks often try to fight back. This is a tempting thing to do, because it can make a government look strong. It can add to its popularity at home, and deter future terrorist attacks. However, direct military action against terrorist groups is difficult, because the terrorists usually work under cover. They also work in self-contained cells far apart from each other. Even if one cell is destroyed, the organization can continue to function. Because terrorists are usually so well hidden, countries often find it easier to put pressure on the sponsors of terrorism rather than attacking the terrorists themselves.

▼ *The funeral of victims of the 1986 U.S. bombing of Tripoli, Libya. The U.S. raid was in retaliation for a Libyan-backed terrorist attack on U.S. soldiers in West Berlin, Germany.*

"We must fight terror wherever and whenever it appears. We must make all states play by the same rules. We must declare terrorism a crime against humanity, and we must consider the terrorists enemies of mankind...."

Benjamin Netanyahu, former Prime Minister of Israel, from the foreword to his book Fighting Terrorism *(2001)*

Another way of fighting terrorists is by blocking off their sources of weapons and arms. The United States and several other countries have antiterrorism laws that make it a crime to give money or materials to terrorist organizations. The authorities can expel suspected terrorists from the country and ban the manufacture or possession of weapons of mass destruction.

When taking action against suspected terrorists, great care must be taken not to affect the rights and freedoms of all citizens. The methods used include surveillance, imprisonment without trial, even torture. When striking at terrorists there is a serious risk of killing innocent civilians. These tactics can play into the terrorists' hands by making the government unpopular. However, nondemocratic governments, such as Iran, that do not depend on the votes of the general public to remain in power, have used these tactics effectively against terrorists.

▲ *Captured terrorists from the al-Qaeda terrorist group are held at Camp Delta in Guantanamo Bay, Cuba in 2002. The use of chains, goggles, and face masks led to international concern that the United States was mistreating these prisoners.*

Talking to terrorists

Governments often decide that the only answer to terrorism is to sit down and talk with the terrorists to try to end the violence. However, negotiation has its drawbacks. For example, France has made deals with terrorists, offering money and political concessions in order to protect Paris from bomb attacks and to get hostages released. This might save lives and property in the short term, but it risks encouraging terrorists to keep doing the same thing. In 1993 France released Iranian terrorists from prison, hoping this would persuade Iran to stop killing its enemies living in France. However, the killings actually increased after this.

◀ *Belfast residents get their first look at the "Good Friday" peace agreement signed in April 1998 by the British and Irish governments, the Unionists, and Sinn Fein. This agreement was an attempt to put an end to IRA terrorist attacks in Northern Ireland with a peace deal.*

Many countries do not like to admit that they talk to terrorists. The official policy of both Great Britain and the United States is that they do not negotiate with terrorists. Yet during the 1980s, both countries did. Britain negotiated in secret with the IRA, leading to peace talks in 1994. The United States offered weapons to Iran in exchange for the release of American hostages in Lebanon.

Many governments use a mixture of both force and negotiation. They instruct their army and intelligence services to undermine the terrorist threat, but they also negotiate when necessary. Israel attacks terrorist bases in its occupied territories, but it has also made deals with terrorists on a number of occasions. For instance, several hundred Muslim prisoners were released from its jails in exchange for hostages following a hijacking in 1985.

> "Each day without a life being taken is a bonus. I now have a two-and-a-half-year-old daughter and another baby on the way. For their sake I want peace. No principle is worth spilling another drop of Ulster blood for. Life is precious; the nightmare has gone on long enough."
>
> *A Protestant mother from Northern Ireland after the 1994 announcement of an IRA cease-fire, quoted in Laurel Holliday,* Children of "the Troubles": Our Lives in the Crossfire of Northern Ireland, *1997*

▶ *Thirteen Lebanese men, held prisoner in Israel for more than ten years, are freed in April 2000. They were released in exchange for information about Israeli soldiers missing in action in Lebanon.*

Protecting ourselves from terrorism

What can we do to defend ourselves from terrorist attacks? Governments spend millions of dollars each year on security and intelligence. They use secret agents to get inside terrorist networks. They take action against terrorist assets and funding. They protect their leaders from attack and guard their borders.

Getting reliable information about the identity, plans, and weaknesses of terrorists is difficult, but it is vital to any counter-terrorism strategy. Intelligence gathering involves the use of high technology, such as satellite photography and electronic bugging equipment. It also uses the intelligence of the people on the ground, taking advantage of their language skills and local knowledge in politically unstable regions.

◀ *This satellite image shows an al-Qaeda training camp in Afghanistan. It was one of the targets of a 1998 U.S. missile attack against the terrorist group.*

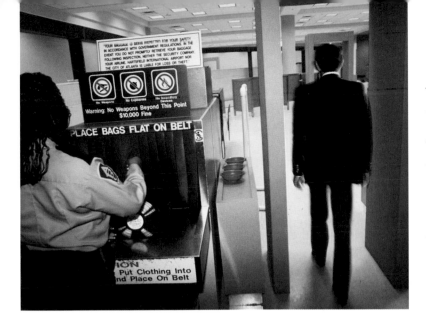

Airplanes are popular targets for terrorist attacks. All international airports search passengers and their luggage for concealed weapons before they are allowed to board a flight.

Cooperation between countries is also vital to counter the threat of terrorism around the world. Governments often work together, signing extradition treaties and sharing intelligence. Nations can also act together by putting pressure on a country that supports terror. For example, they can impose sanctions by refusing to trade with it or by blocking the export of valuable products like oil.

On a personal level, we can also take action to protect ourselves from terrorism in the home, in the street, or while traveling abroad. We can make sure our homes are safe from intruders and properly alarmed, and that we know what to do if we see anything suspicious. We can learn how to recognize suspicious packages and what to do if we think we see one.

FACT:
During the 1990s spending on counter-terrorism rose dramatically in most Western countries. The U.S. annual anti-terrorism budget rose by more than 50 percent between 1996 and 2001, to $10 billion. That figure rose even higher in 2002 when the Federal Bureau of Intelligence (FBI) recruited 900 new agents for counter-terrorism work.

The United Nations and terrorism

The United Nations (UN) is an organization of countries that was established in 1945 for the purpose of promoting international peace, security, and cooperation. Since global terrorism first emerged in the 1960s, the UN has played an important part in getting different countries to agree on how to fight it.

◀ *United Nations weapons inspectors in Iraq in 1998 destroy chemical weapons containing the deadly nerve gas, sarin.*

The UN has held many debates on terrorism and has passed more than 20 antiterrorism treaties and resolutions. These include measures to prevent hijackings, hostage taking, and assassinations. They also include agreements to undermine terrorist activity by restricting the movement of terrorist assets (like money), and banning the financing or arming of (providing weapons to) terrorists. The UN also often acts as a voice for international outrage following terrorist attacks. It condemns such acts, and calls for sanctions against states that support terrorism.

Not all countries agree with such measures, and so the UN has also been the scene of arguments between nations, especially over the definition of terrorism. Many Islamic countries, for example, would like the definition widened to include the actions taken by Israel against Palestinians in the occupied territories.

The UN does not have the political or military power to enforce these resolutions. It relies on the willingness of individual governments to do so. However, it does play a significant role in encouraging action against terrorism.

FACT:
As well as passing treaties and resolutions, the UN also has organizations and agencies to advise on counter-terrorism methods. For example, the International Civil Aviation Organization suggests how best to meet the threat of hijacks; the International Atomic Energy Agency looks at the security of nuclear material in nuclear power plants; and the World Health Organization advises on what to do in the event of a biological weapons attack.

◄ *A chemical weapons expert checks toxicity levels during a training exercise. In 2002 the World Health Organization (WHO) published detailed guidelines on how governments should respond to a biological or chemical weapons attack.*

6. What Is the War on Terrorism?

What happened on September 11, 2001?

Tuesday, September 11, 2001 saw the most devastating terrorist attack in history. Two hijacked aircraft crashed into the north and south towers of the World Trade Center in New York City, causing both towers to collapse. A third plane crashed into the Pentagon in Washington, D.C., and a fourth hijacked plane crash-landed in Pennsylvania, killing everyone on board (this plane was probably headed for the White House). In this carefully planned attack on the symbols of American military and economic power, more than 3,000 people died.

▼ *This photo, taken at 9:03 A.M., shows Flight 175, with 65 passengers and crew on board, about to crash into the south tower of the World Trade Center.*

The terrorist organization responsible was al-Qaeda, a powerful and very secretive network of Islamic fundamentalist cells coordinated by Osama bin Laden. September 11 appeared to be the awful fulfilment of bin Laden's 1998 fatwah (ruling) calling on Muslims to kill Americans. People in the United States were shocked that such an attack could happen in one of the best-defended countries on earth. Many realized for the first time that modern-day terrorism is ruthless and can strike anywhere.

One of the most alarming aspects of the September 11 attack was its simplicity. No weapons of mass destruction or high-tech gadgetry were used. The attack was carried out by a group of terrorists, some of them with piloting skills, armed with small knives who were prepared to sacrifice their lives for their cause. It has raised doubts about many aspects of U.S. defense, including failures in intelligence and domestic airport security in the United States and other countries.

▲ *More than 300 firefighters died during the destruction of the World Trade Center.*

case study·case study·case study·case study·case study

Mohammed Atta was one of the pilots who flew an aircraft into the World Trade Center. He was possibly the ringleader of the whole attack. He was born in 1968, the son of a successful lawyer, and grew up in a wealthy neighborhood in Cairo, Egypt. He moved to Germany to study architecture in 1993. Intelligent and well-educated, he did not fit the description of a typical terrorist. Yet his fellow students in Hamburg recall that Atta grew more and more religious during his time there. He started an Islamic prayer group in 1999, which may have been a recruiting place for Islamic militants. He moved to the United States in 2001, where he studied aviation at a Florida flying school. On the morning of September 11, he and a colleague traveled to Boston and boarded American Airlines Flight 11. In his diary Atta prepared himself for the moment of his death: "You should feel complete tranquillity, because the time between you and your marriage in heaven is very short."

The military war

The events of September 11, 2001, may have marked a turning point in history. They have led to great changes in Western foreign policy, especially in Western ways of dealing with terrorism. In the weeks and months following the attacks, The United States and its allies began a "War on Terrorism." Several old enemies from the Cold War era, such as the United States, Russia, and China, have found themselves working together to combat terrorism.

In October 2001 the United States led an attack on al-Qaeda bases in Afghanistan and against the Taliban, the Islamic fundamentalist rulers of Afghanistan who refused to hand over Osama bin Laden. By December, the Taliban government in Afghanistan had been overthrown, but the fight against al-Qaeda continued.

▼ *Two soldiers from the Afghan rebel force, the Northern Alliance, watch as U.S. B-52 bombers attack Taliban positions in northern Afghanistan in November 2001.*

▲ U.S. and Canadian soldiers conduct a raid to destroy al-Qaeda positions in Afghanistan.

By June al-Qaeda forces had split into small groups in different parts of the country, making it difficult to find and defeat them. Bin Laden and his top leaders were not found.

Early in 2002 the United States turned its attention to other places where al-Qaeda cells were believed to exist, such as in Pakistan, Georgia, Yemen, Sudan, Somalia, Iraq, and the Philippines. For this next stage in the war on terror, American forces, including CIA agents, were used to advise, train, and provide intelligence and technical assistance to each country. Troops were also able to carry out carefully targeted raids on suspected terrorist cells.

> "The main problem in the last three months of war has been that while the United States has destroyed al-Qaeda's terror network, it has not eradicated its members."
>
> *General Juraat Khan Panjshiri, Afghanistan's national security chief, speaking in May 2002*

The war on terrorist funds

A war against funding for terrorists also began after September 11. A few weeks after the attacks, the UN passed Resolution 1373, its most wide-ranging antiterrorism measure to date. The countries that signed the resolution agreed to ban the supply of money or arms to known terrorists. They also agreed to freeze terrorist assets in their banks and to deny a safe haven to terrorists or those who support them. Border controls to restrict the movement of terrorists were introduced. They also promised to give early warning of possible future terrorist acts to other countries.

The United States has led the campaign to root out terrorist cells. It has become evident that these cells exist in many of the major cities of Europe and North America. Between September 2001 and March 2002, about 1,000 suspected terrorists were arrested, and at least $80 million in terrorist assets were frozen by more than 140 countries. Even former terrorist-supporting countries like Libya and Sudan have offered to share information on the al-Qaeda network with the United States.

▲ Mohammed Atta at the Maine airport on September 11, 2001. Later that morning he would lead the hijackers on American Airlines Flight 11.

◀ U.S. customs officers raid a bank in Minneapolis, Minnesota in November 2001. The bank was suspected of playing a part in al-Qaeda's worldwide money-transfer network.

Another focus of the War on Terrorism is the world banking system. Modern electronic banking allows large sums of money to flow between bank accounts around the world within a matter of minutes. This makes it easy for terrorist leaders to pay their agents in different countries. A combination of poor business practice and corruption has also allowed terrorists to take advantage of this system for money laundering. In November 2001 the International Monetary Fund (IMF) urged its members to set up "financial intelligence squads" to look out for suspicious dealings.

FACT:
In March 2002 a joint U.S.-Saudi Arabian operation was carried out to freeze the assets of al-Haramain Islamic Foundation, a charitable organization accused by the United States of using its funds to support terrorist groups including al-Qaeda and the Somalia-based al-Itihaad al-Islamiya. U.S. Treasury Secretary Paul O'Neill called the operation "a sign of the growing strength of the antiterror coalition."

Terrorists of tomorrow

The war against terrorism is about confronting not only terrorist groups but also the countries that sponsor them. Some Western countries, particularly the United States, are worried about the possibility that anti-Western regimes might supply terrorists with weapons of mass destruction.

In 2002 the U.S. government expressed its concern that Saddam Hussein's Iraq was developing such weapons, in violation of United Nations resolutions. The United States argued that Iraq had links with al-Qaeda, although there was no evidence for this, and that it was only a matter of time before these dangerous weapons were used against Western targets.

In November 2002 the UN adopted Resolution 1441 demanding that Iraq provide a record of its weapons of mass destruction, and allow access to

▼ Iraqis surrender to coalition troops during the Iraq War of 2003. The U.S. and British governments insisted their quarrel was with Saddam Hussein, not the people of Iraq. Nevertheless, many Arabs were angered by the invasion, which they saw as an act of Western aggression against a much weaker Arab country.

◀ *Osama bin Laden, who avoided capture in the U.S.-led attack on Afghanistan, spoke to the world in several videos released in late 2001 and early 2002. He remains a hero to many radical young Muslims around the world.*

its weapons sites by an inspection team. Iraq failed to comply with these demands, and in March 2003, U.S. and British forces invaded Iraq. Within weeks, Saddam's regime was toppled. The invasion, and the loss of civilian life it caused, angered many Arabs. It is currently unclear what effect the war in Iraq will have on terrorism or the War on Terrorism.

Since September 11, the world has awakened to the threat of terrorism. Countries are working together to confront this threat. As well as remaining watchful for future attacks, governments must also try to put an end to the conflicts that breed new generations of terrorists.

FACT:
Cyber-terrorism is the name given to terrorist attacks on computer systems. These could be used to disrupt essential services such as transportation, hospitals, and police. Cyber-terrorist weapons include devices that use microwaves to destroy electronics. Electromagnetic bombs can create shock waves up to a thousand times stronger than a lightning strike. More common are computer viruses, which attack computer systems by planting harmful programs into them.

GLOSSARY

anarchist
one who does not believe in the need for government

arson
crime of purposely setting fire to a building or other property

assassination
deliberate killing of a public figure, such as a political or military leader

biological weapon
missile, bomb, or other device used to deliver and spread biological agents that cause disease or death to humans, plants, and animals

capitalism
economic system based on the private ownership of wealth, characterized by a free market and motivated by profit

cell
small group of people who work together. They are often part of a larger group, such as a terrorist organization, but operate independently of other cells.

Chechen
native Muslim person of Chechnia, a republic in southwestern Russia. Chechen guerrillas are fighting for their independence from Russia.

chemical weapon
missile, bomb, or other device used to deliver and spread chemical agents, such as a nerve gas or a poison to injure or kill humans, plants, and animals

Christian Democrat Party
conservative political party in Italy. It was the dominant power in most of Italy's governments between 1945 and 1981.

Central Intelligence Agency (CIA)
U.S. government agency responsible for intelligence and counter-intelligence activities outside the United States

coalition
temporary alliance between two or more groups, such as countries or political parties

Cold War
state of nonviolent conflict between the Soviet Union and the United States and their respective allies between 1945 and 1990

communism
political system in which all property and wealth is controlled by the state

computer virus
computer program, usually hidden within another harmless-looking program, that damages a computer system, for example, by destroying data

counter-terrorism
military or political activities intended to combat or prevent terrorism

cyber-terrorism
form of terrorism in which computer systems are attacked or threatened

democratic
system of government that is ruled by the will of the people. Often used to describe a state in which everyone has equal rights.

ethnic
relating to a group of people who share the same origins and culture

extradition
handing over by a government of somebody accused of a crime to a different country for trial or punishment there

fatwah
formal religious ruling issued by an Islamic leader

foreign policy
program adopted by a government that defines its attitudes and actions toward other countries and their governments

freedom fighter
positive name for one who takes part in an armed uprising against a political system, government, or occupying power that he or she opposes

French Revolution
period of violent political upheaval in France (1789–1799). During this time the French monarchy was overthrown.

fundamentalism
religious movement based on a strict interpretation of holy writings

guillotine
machine for cutting off people's heads

hijack
forcefully take control of a vehicle, such as an airplane, train, or bus

International Monetary Fund
agency of the United Nations that seeks to promote international cooperation between countries on financial matters

investment
outlay of money with the object of making a profit, or in the hope of getting a benefit from it

left-wing
in politics, supporting the idea that the government is responsible for creating social change; also used to describe people or beliefs that are not bound by tradition

militants
people who actively support a cause, sometimes using violent methods to achieve their aims

money laundering
passing illegally obtained money through a legal business or bank account to hide its origins

nationalism
feeling that people in a country or area all belong together and are different from people in other

places. Also used to describe a belief in the superiority of your own country or ethnicity.

nuclear weapon
missile or bomb with massive explosive power based on nuclear fission, the splitting of an atom's nucleus into smaller fragments

opium
drug derived from the brownish extract from the unripe seedpods of a kind of poppy. It contains highly addictive substances such as morphine. The morphine in opium is used in the manufacture of heroin.

oppressive
harsh or cruelly dominating

patriotism
pride in one's country

radioactive
emitting energy in the form of streams of particles, due to the decaying of unstable atoms. Elements such as uranium and plutonium are radioactive.

Real IRA
splinter group of the IRA (Irish Republican Army) formed in 1998. The Real IRA is opposed to the peace process and the IRA ceasefire in Northern Ireland. They are dedicated to removing British forces from Northern Ireland using violent means.

resolution
agreement intending to make peace between conflicting sides in a dispute

right-wing
in politics, supporting the idea that social change and reform are not generally part of government's role; also used to describe people or beliefs that are more bound by tradition

sanctions
measures taken by one or more nations to apply pressure on another nation to conform to international opinion, for example, by ending trade with it

sarin
extremely poisonous gas that attacks a person's central nervous system, causing convulsions and often death

satellite photography
pictures taken by spy satellites that orbit the earth

Soviet Union
federation of communist states, including Russia, that existed in eastern Europe and north and central Asia from 1917 to 1991

state-sponsored terrorism
terrorism that is supported by governments. Sponsorship can include the giving of funds, weapons, equipment, training or protection.

strategy
carefully worked-out plan of action to achieve a goal, such as victory in a war

surveillance
continued observation of a person or group of people

treaty
formal contract or agreement that is negotiated between countries and signed by all the parties involved

weapons of mass destruction
chemical, biological, and nuclear weapons

World Health Organization (WHO) agency of the United Nations that helps countries improve their health services and coordinates international action against diseases and other threats to health

FURTHER INFORMATION

BOOKS TO READ

Bingley, Richard. *Terrorism*. Chicago: Raintree, 2004.
Daley, Patric. *9.11.01: Terrorists Attack*. Chicago: Raintree, 2003.
Downing, David. *Iraq: 1968-2003*. Chicago: Raintree, 2004.
Downing, David. *The War on Terrorism: The First Year*. Chicago: Raintree, 2004.
Frank, Mitch. *Understanding September 11th: Answering Questions About the Attacks on America*. New York: Viking, 2002.
Meltzer, Milton. *The Day the Sky Fell: A History of Terrorism*. New York: Random House, 2002.
Minnis, Ivan. *The Arab-Israeli Conflict*. Chicago: Raintree, 2003.
Minnis, Ivan. *Troubles in Northern Ireland*. Chicago: Raintree, 2003.
Woolf, Alex. *21st Century Debates: Terrorism*. Chicago: Raintree, 2004.

INDEX